W9-ADH-700

DK READERS

Level 2

Dinosaur Dinners
Fire Fighter!
Bugs! Bugs! Bugs!
Slinky, Scaly Snakes!
Animal Hospital
The Little Ballerina
Munching, Crunching, Sniffing, and Snooping
The Secret Life of Trees
Winking, Blinking, Wiggling, and Waggling
Astronaut: Living in Space
Twisters!
Holiday! Celebration Days around the World
The Story of Pocahontas
Horse Show
Survivors: The Night the Titanic Sank
Eruption! The Story of Volcanoes
The Story of Columbus
Journey of a Humpback Whale
Amazing Buildings
Feathers, Flippers, and Feet
Outback Adventure: Australian Vacation
Sniffles, Sneezes, Hiccups, and Coughs
¡Insectos! *en español*
¡Bomberos! *en español*
Ice Skating Stars
Let's Go Riding!
LEGO: Castle Under Attack
LEGO: Rocket Rescue
Star Wars: Journey Through Space
MLB: A Batboy's Day
MLB: Let's Go to the Ballpark!
Spider-Man: Worst Enemies
Meet the X-Men

Level 3

Spacebusters: The Race to the Moon
Beastly Tales
Shark Attack!
Titanic
Invaders from Outer Space
Movie Magic
Plants Bite Back!
Time Traveler
Bermuda Triangle
Tiger Tales
Aladdin
Heidi
Zeppelin: The Age of the Airship
Spies
Terror on the Amazon
Disasters at Sea
The Story of Anne Frank
Abraham Lincoln: Lawyer, Leader, Legend
George Washington: Soldier, Hero, President
Extreme Sports
Spiders' Secrets
The Big Dinosaur Dig
Space Heroes: Amazing Astronauts
The Story of Chocolate
Abraham Lincoln: Abogado, Líder, Leyenda *en español*
Al Espacio: La Carrera a la Luna *en español*
LEGO: Mission to the Arctic
NFL: Super Bowl Heroes
NFL: Peyton Manning
NFL: Whiz Kid Quarterbacks
MLB: Home Run Heroes: Big Mac, Sammy, and Junior
MLB: Roberto Clemente
MLB: Roberto Clemente *en español*
MLB: World Series Heroes
MLB: Record Breakers
MLB: Down to the Wire: Baseball's Great Pennant Races
Star Wars: Star Pilot
The X-Men School

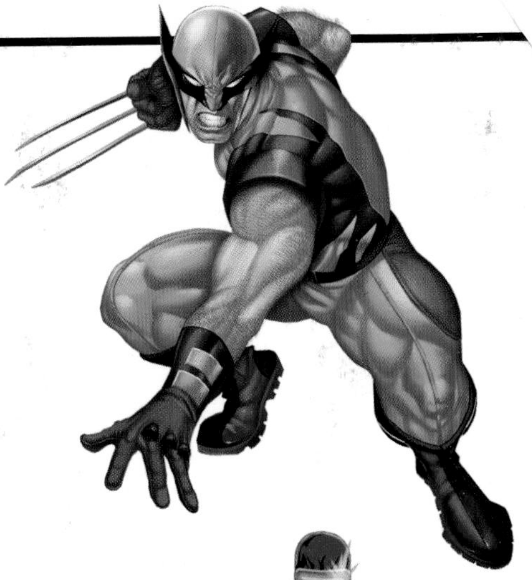

LONDON, NEW YORK, MUNICH,
MELBOURNE, AND DELHI

For DK Publishing
Editor Kate Simkins
Designer Mika Kean-Hammerson
Design Manager Rob Perry
Publishing Manager Simon Beecroft
Category Publisher Alex Allan
DTP Designer Lauren Egan
Production Rochelle Talary

For Marvel
Editors Mickey Stern and Carl Suecoff

Reading Consultant
Linda B. Gambrell

First American Edition, 2006
Published in the United States by
DK Publishing, Inc.
375 Hudson Street
New York, New York 10014

06 07 08 10 10 9 8 7 6 5 4 3 2 1

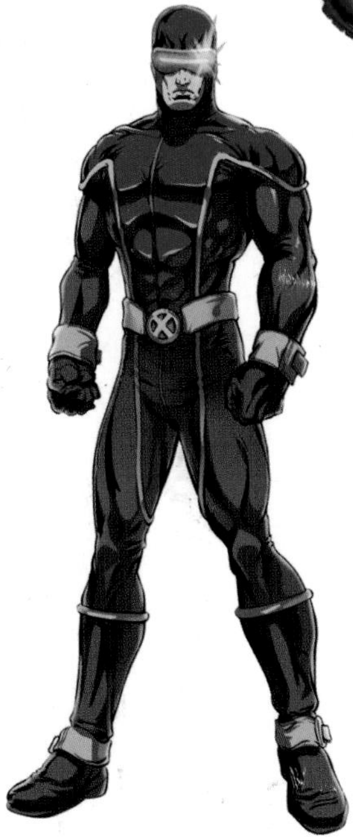

Published in Great Britain by Dorling Kindersley Limited.

A catalog reccord for this book is available from the
Library of Congress.

ISBN 13: 978-0-75661-928-2 (paperback)
ISBN 10: 0-7566-1928-9 (paperback)
ISBN 13: 978-0-75661-927-5 (hardcover)
ISBN 0-7566-1927-0 (hardcover)

Color reproduction by Media Development and Printing, UK
Printed and bound by L. Rex Printing Co. Ltd, China

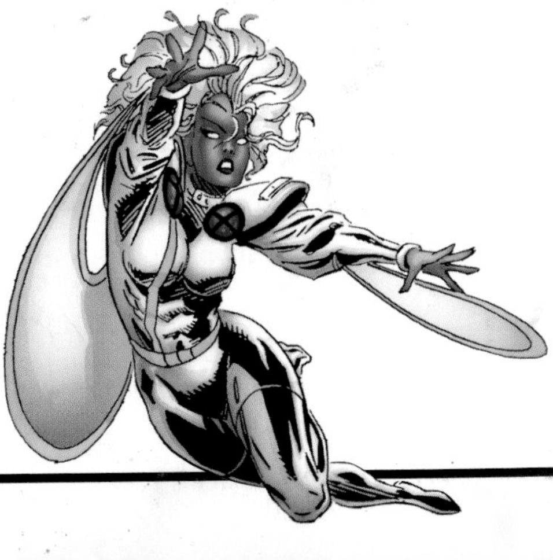

Discover more at
www.dk.com

A Note to Parents and Teachers

DK READERS is a compelling reading program for children, designed in conjunction with leading literacy experts, including Dr. Linda Gambrell, Professor of Education at Clemson University. Dr. Gambrell has served as President of the National Reading Conference, College Reading Association, and has recently been elected to serve as President of the International Reading Association.

Beautiful illustrations and superb full-color photographs combine with engaging, easy-to-read stories to offer a fresh approach to each subject in the series.

Each DK READER is guaranteed to capture a child's interest while developing his or her reading skills, general knowledge, and love of reading.

The five levels of DK READERS are aimed at different reading abilities, enabling you to choose the books that are exactly right for your child:

Pre-level 1 – Learning to read

Level 1 – Beginning to read

Level 2 – Beginning to read alone

Level 3 – Reading alone

Level 4 – Proficient readers

The "normal" age at which a child begins to read can be anywhere from three to eight years old, so these levels are only a general guideline.

No matter which level you select, you can be sure that you are helping your child learn to read, then read to learn!

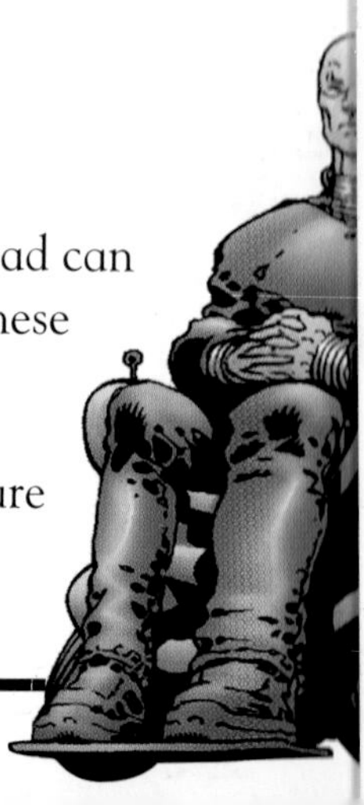

DK READERS

Beginning 2 To Read Alone

Meet the
X-MEN®

Written by Clare Hibbert

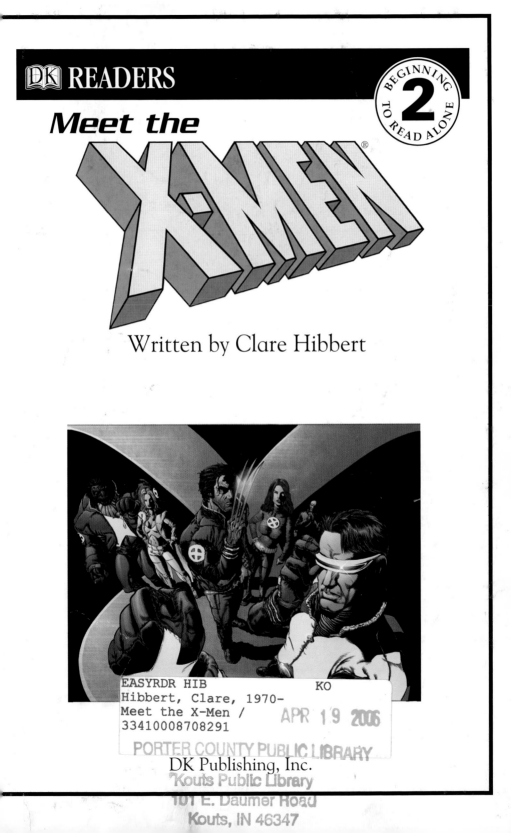

DK Publishing, Inc.

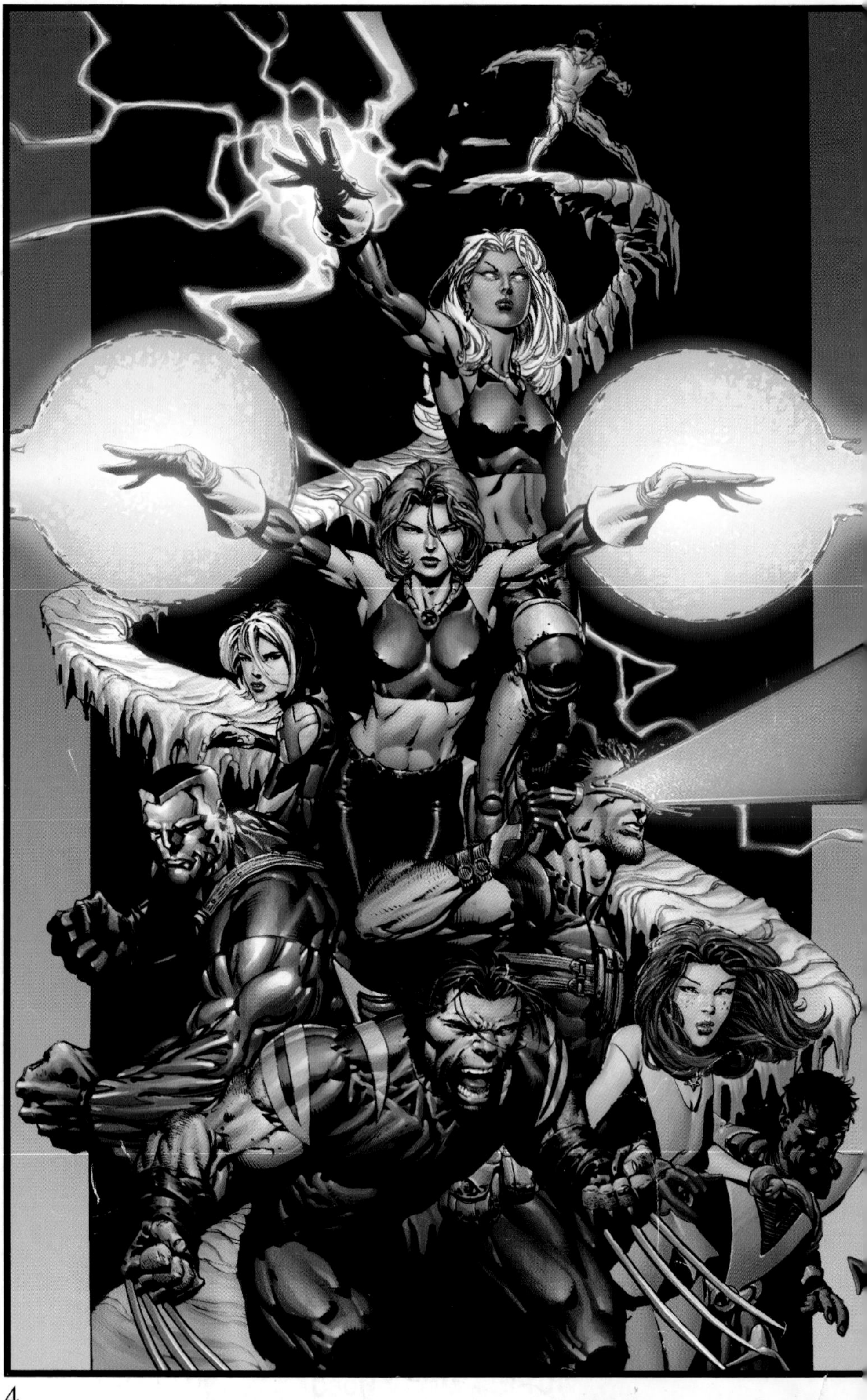

Welcome to the world of
the X-Men.
In this world, there are
some humans who seem ordinary
until they become teenagers.

Then, their special powers appear.
These teenagers are mutants,
also known as the X-Men.

A few humans like the X-Men and
hope that one day everyone will
have special powers.
But most humans fear the X-Men
because they are different
from humans.

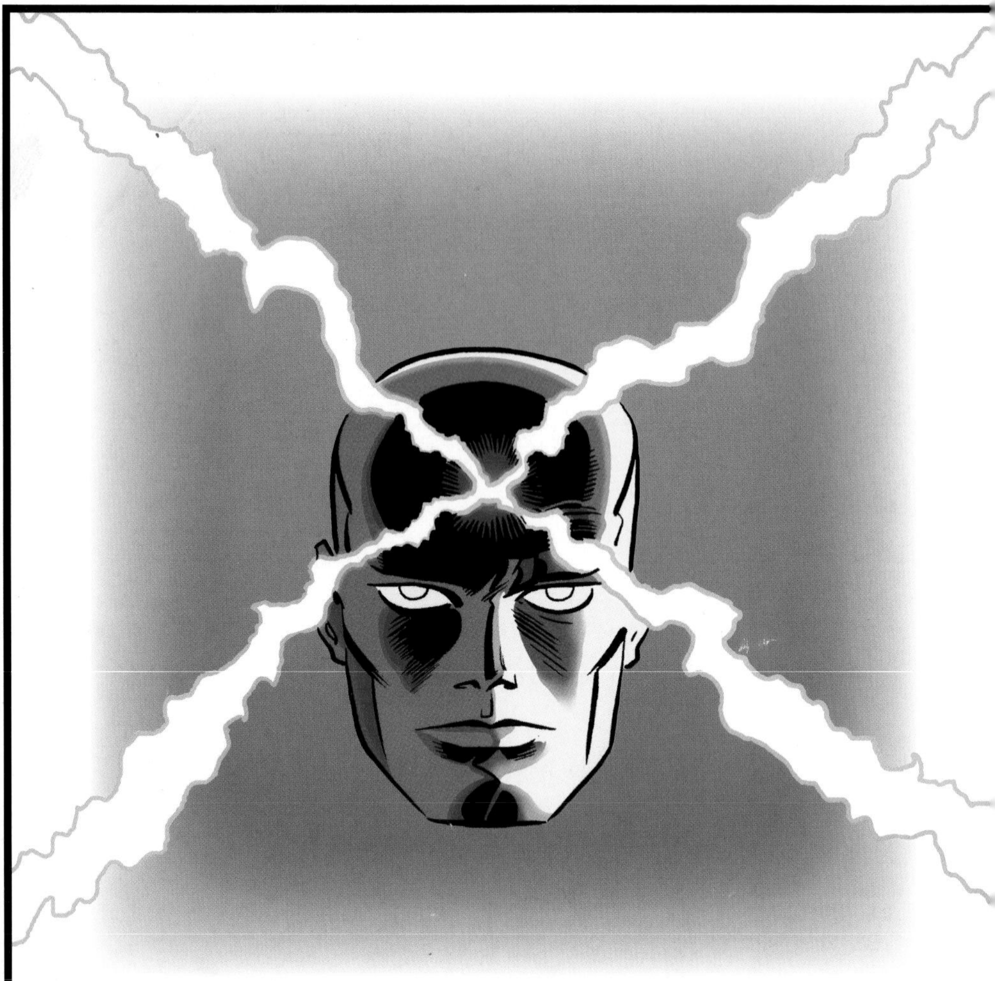

Professor X is the world's top expert on mutants.
He is a mutant himself and has the power to read minds.

Professor X started a school where young mutants could learn to use their powers for good.

He called his students the X-Men.

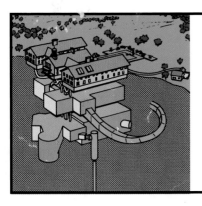

Special school
Professor X's school
is no ordinary school.
It has many secrets.
There is even
an aircraft runway.

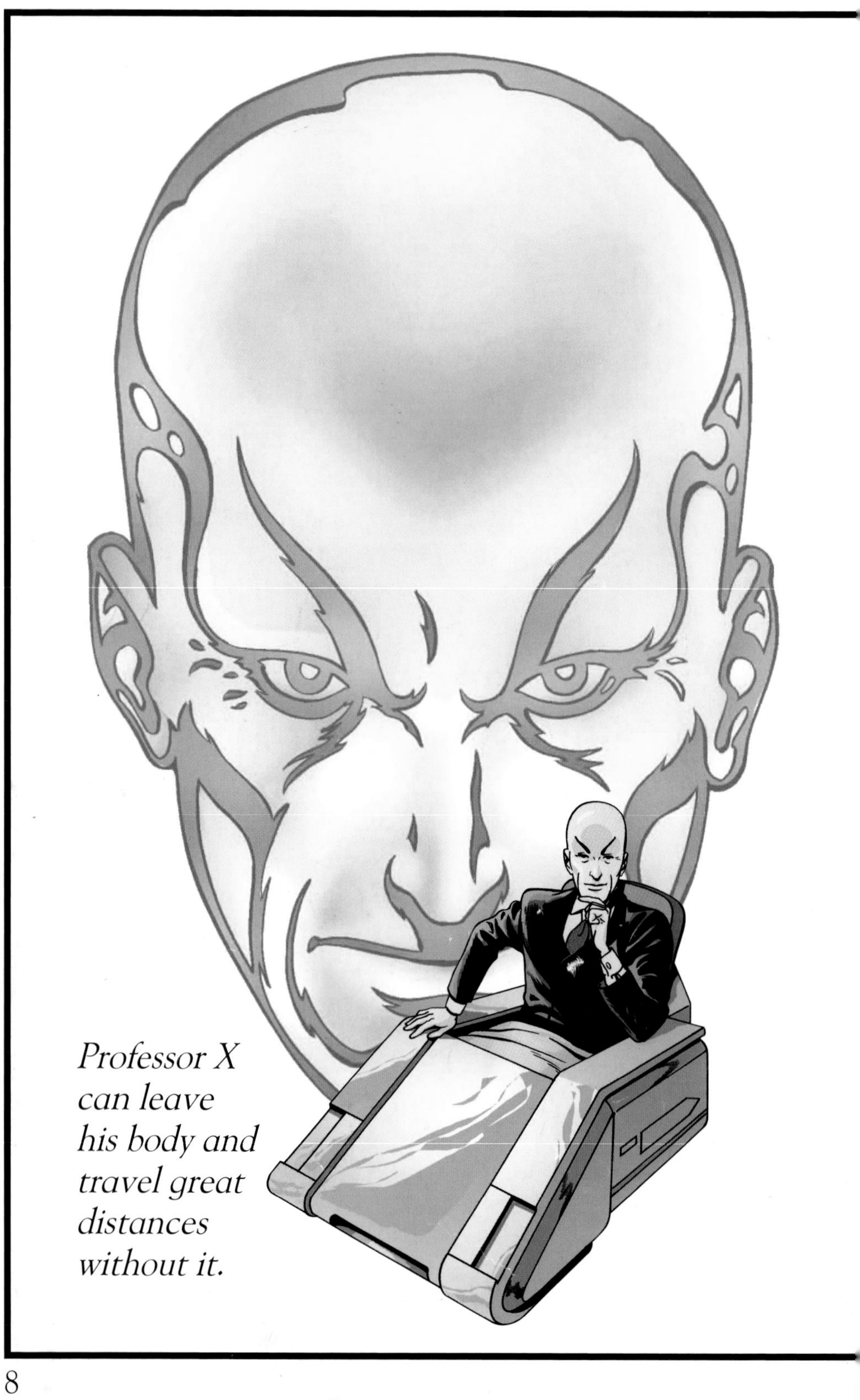

Professor X can leave his body and travel great distances without it.

Professor X wants humans and
mutants to live together in peace.
As a young man, he was crippled in
a battle with the evil alien Lucifer.

*Professor X and
Lucifer fighting.*

Now, he moves around in
a special hoverchair that floats
just above the ground.
Professor X can send messages
into people's minds.

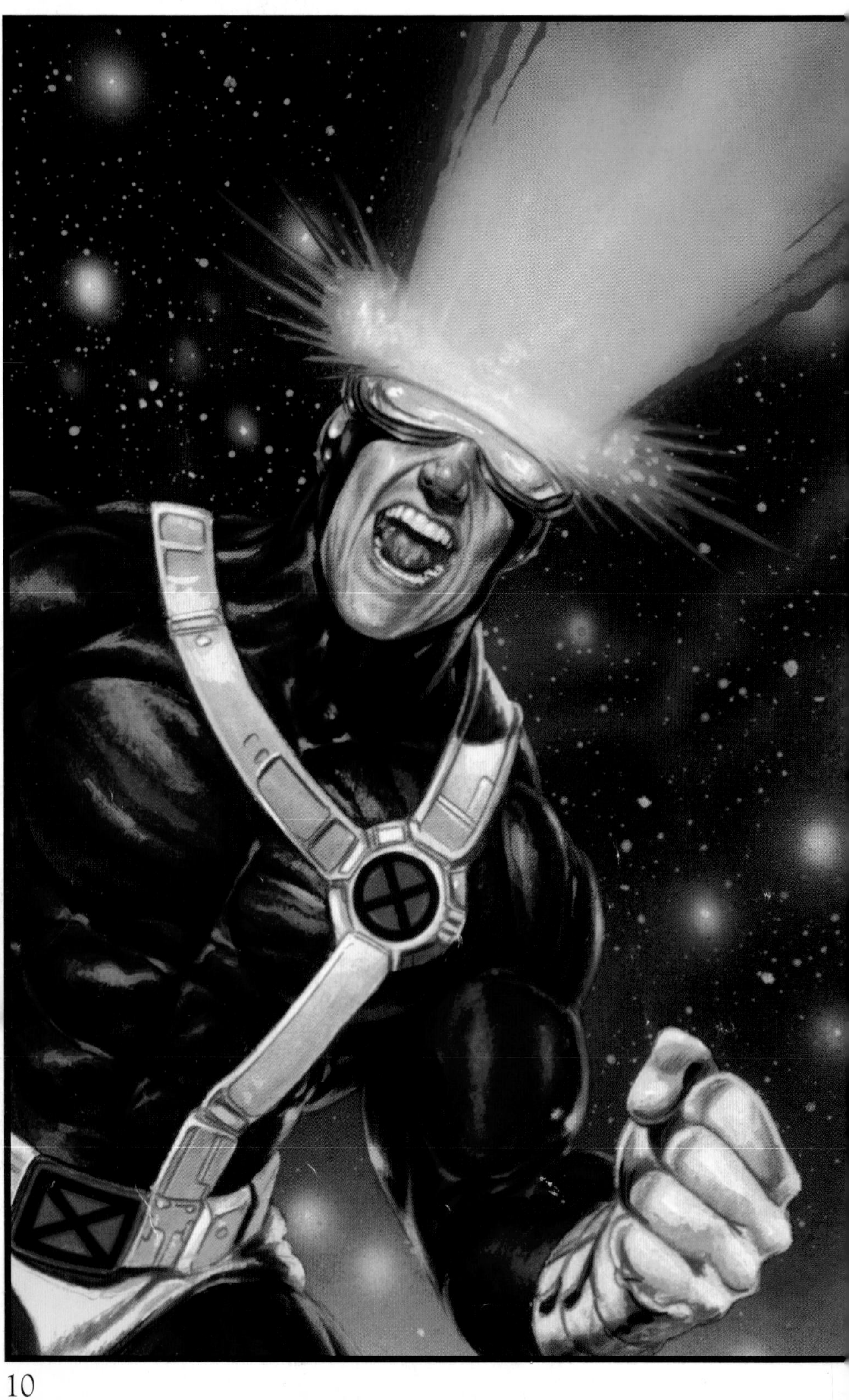

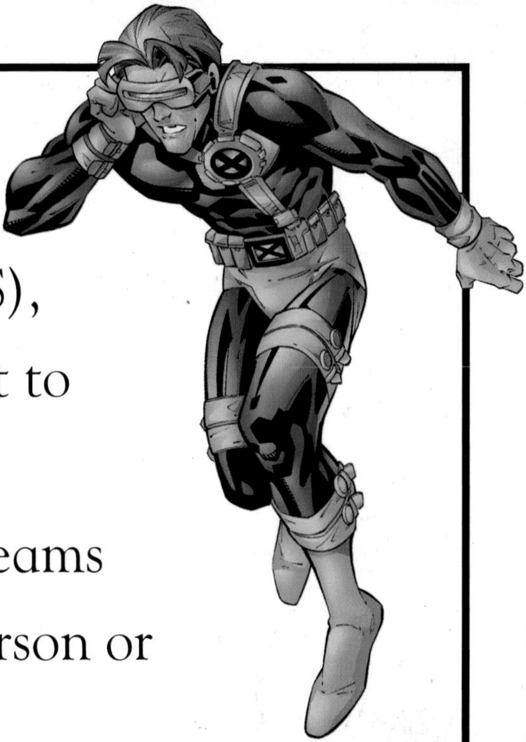

Scott Summers, or Cyclops (SI-CLOPS), was the first mutant to join the X-Men.
His eyes send out beams that can harm a person or blow up a tank.
Cyclops wears special glasses to cover his eyes.

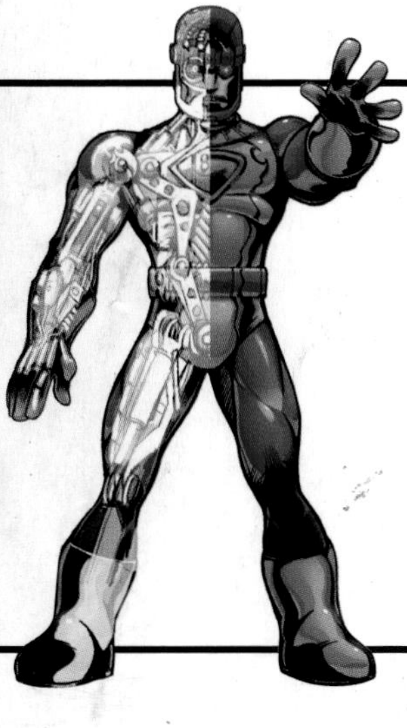

Sentinels
The Sentinels are big robots that were built to destroy mutants.
They fire deadly beams from their eyes like Cyclops.

Jean Grey can move things just by thinking about it.

Jean Grey can read minds like Professor X.
She can also make objects move without touching them.

Jean nearly died from deadly sun rays while flying a spaceship.
When she recovered, she became Phoenix (FEE-NICKS).
She can use a source of energy called the Phoenix Force.

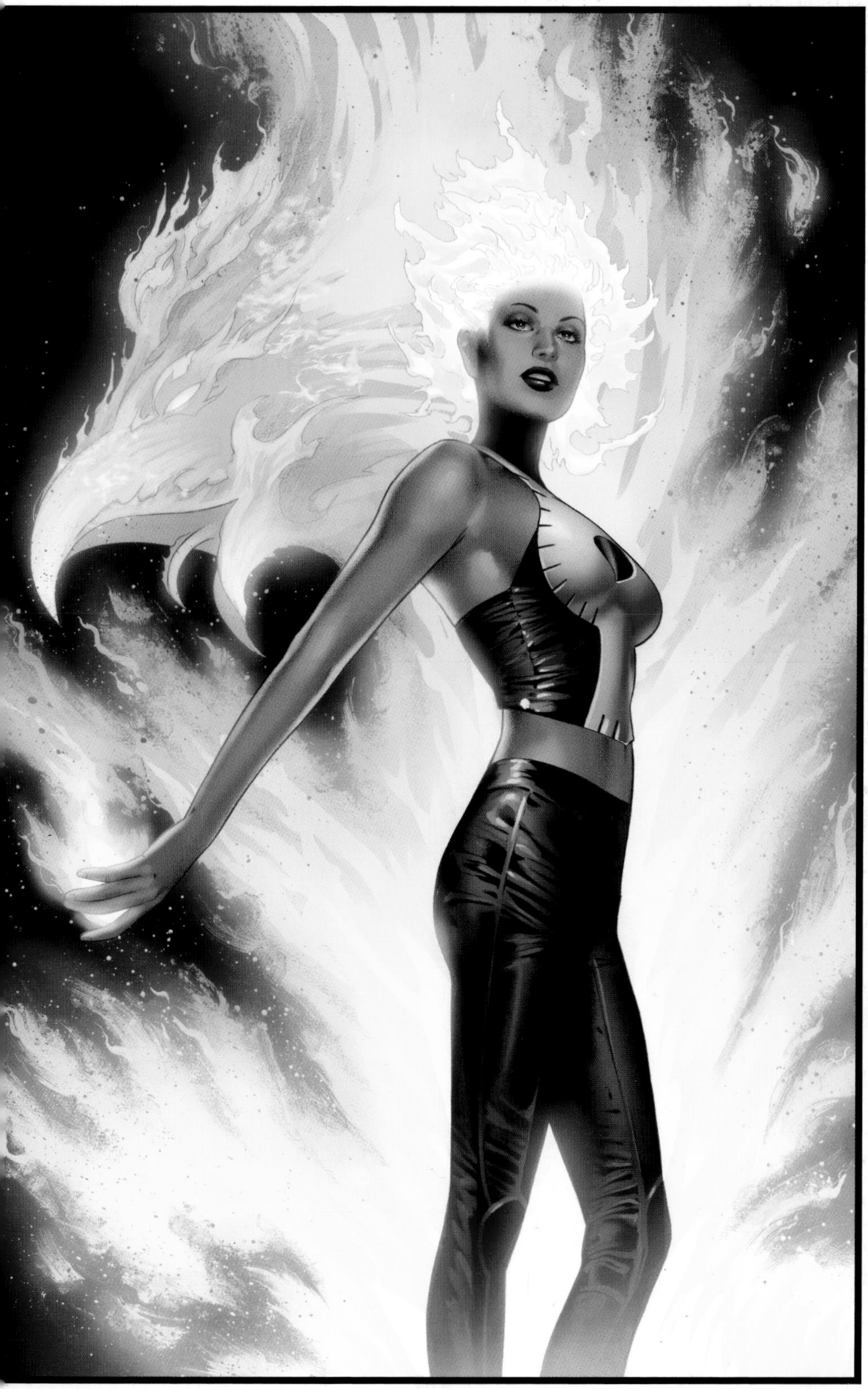

Archangel (ARK-ANGEL) can fly like a bird.

He lost his first wings after a battle with a group of mutant fighters, the Marauders (MA-RAW-DERS).

The X-Men's enemy Apocalypse
(A-POCK-A-LIPS) gave Archangel
a new pair of metal wings.
He became one of Apocalypse's
fighters for a while.

High fliers
The other X-Men
do not have wings.
They fly superfast
jet planes called
Blackbirds.

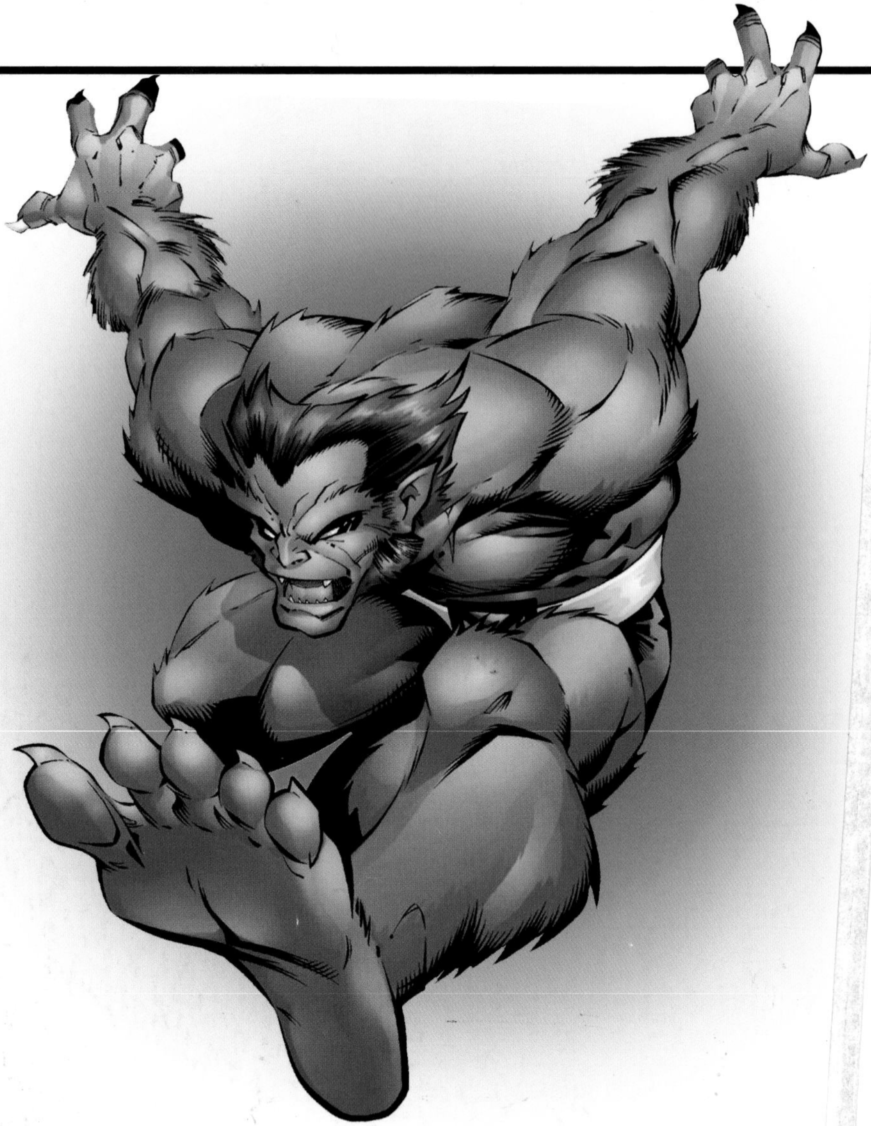

Hank McCoy, known as the Beast, is a clever scientist, but he looks like a furry, blue ape.
He jumps and swings like a chimp and has the strength of a gorilla.

When he was born, Hank seemed ordinary, except for his enormous hands and feet.

He changed into a beast when he drank a strange potion that he made in his laboratory.

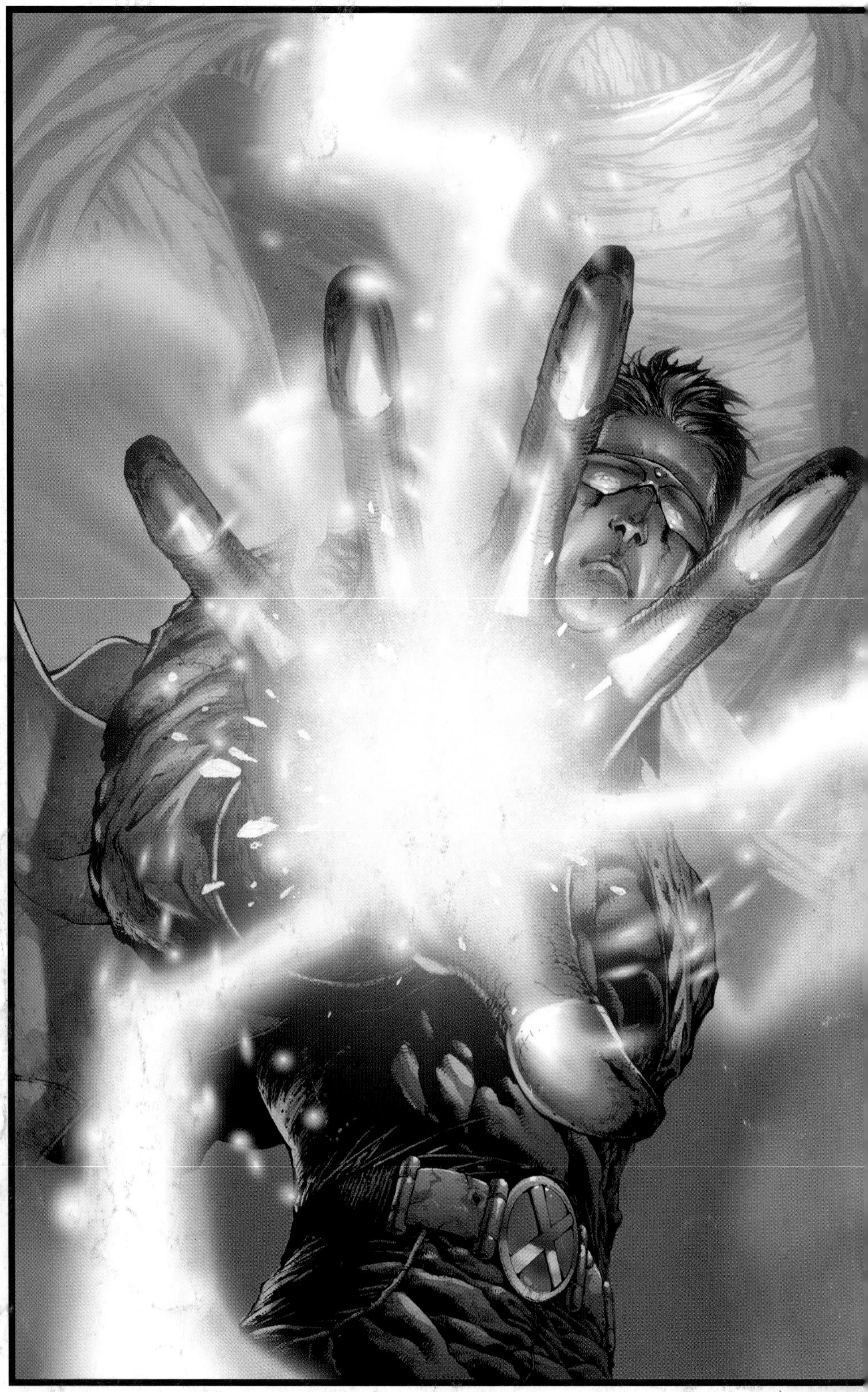

Iceman can turn anything into ice, even his own body.
He can become an ice giant and fire weapons made of ice.
Iceman has a speedy way to get around.
He makes a slippery ice path in front of him and slides along.

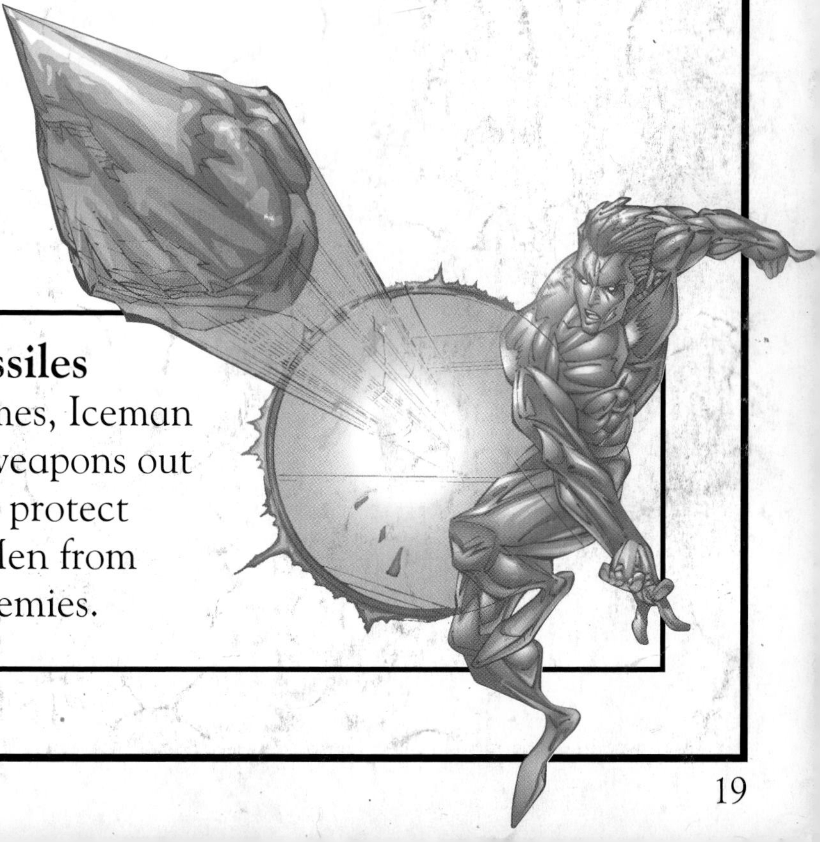

Ice missiles
Sometimes, Iceman makes weapons out of ice to protect the X-Men from their enemies.

Nightcrawler has dark blue skin, yellow eyes, and a pointed tail. He grew up in a circus and was an amazing acrobat even before his super powers appeared.

Nightcrawler can teleport, which means he can move to another place in a second.
He can travel up to three miles (five kilometers).

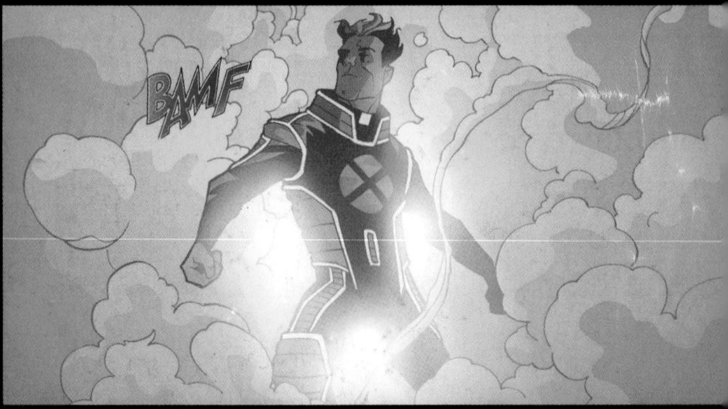
BAMF

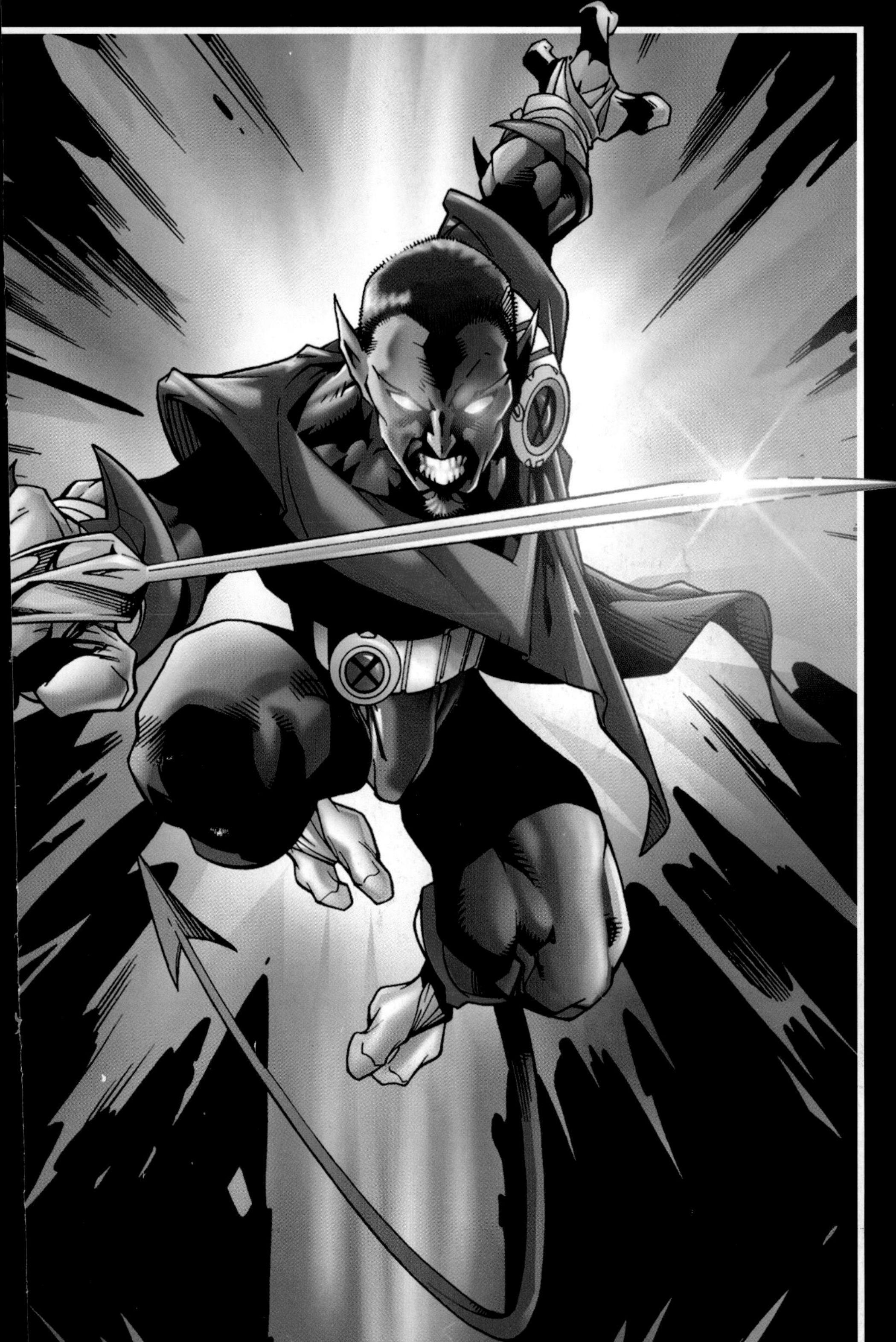

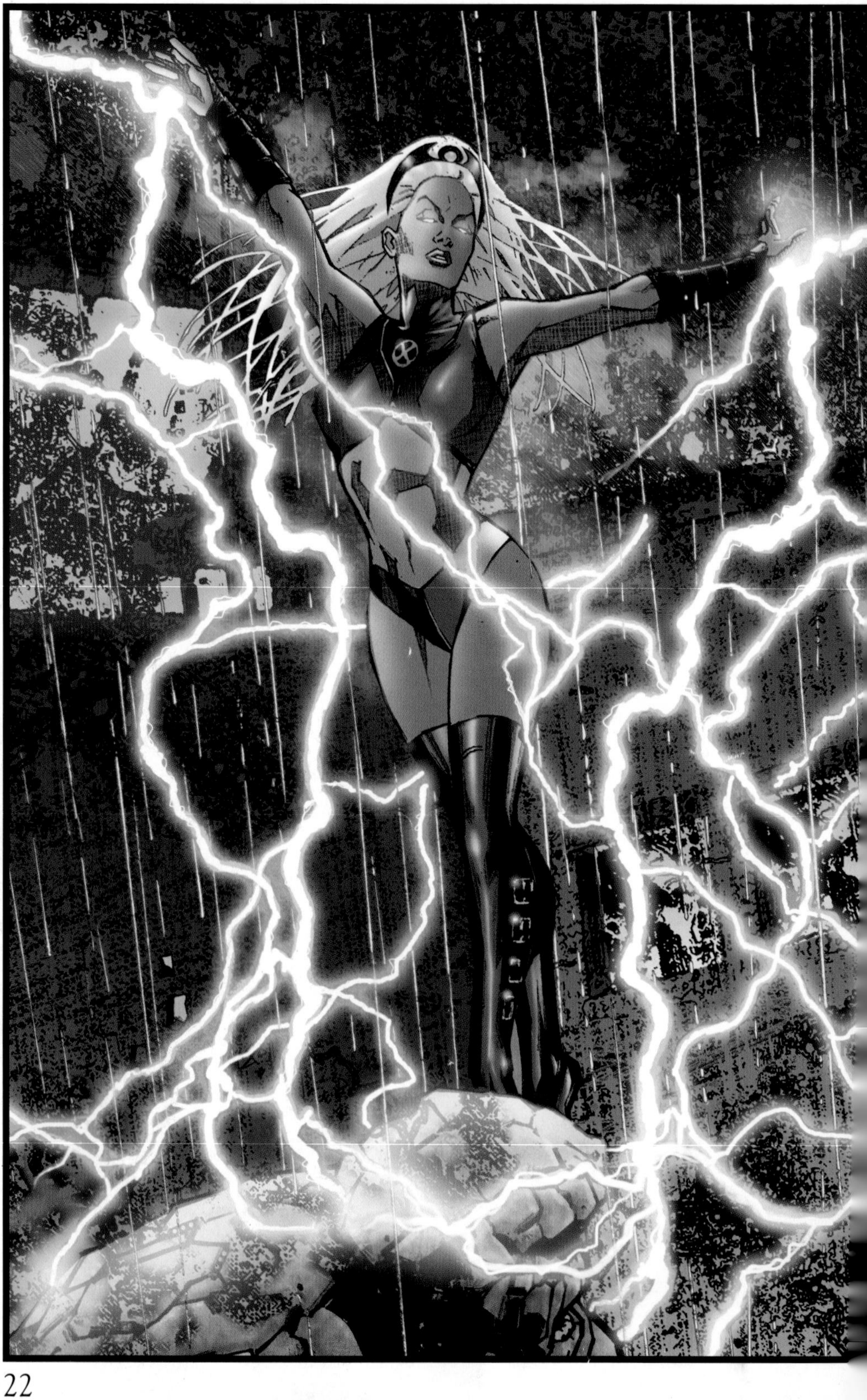

Professor X found Storm in Kenya, Africa, and asked her to join the X-Men.

Storm can create rain, hail, snow, and strong winds.

She can blast lightning bolts from her fingertips.

Useful gift
When she lived in Kenya, Storm used her powers to make rain to help farmers grow their crops. Because of this, the local people worshiped her as a goddess.

Professor X asked Wolverine
(WOOL-VER-EEN) to join
the X-Men.

He is a fierce fighter with
sharp claws and
superhuman hearing.

Wolverine can track a person
by smell, just like a dog.

Sharp claws
Wolverine's claws
are made of very
strong metal.
He can push them
out of his knuckles
whenever he needs
to use them.

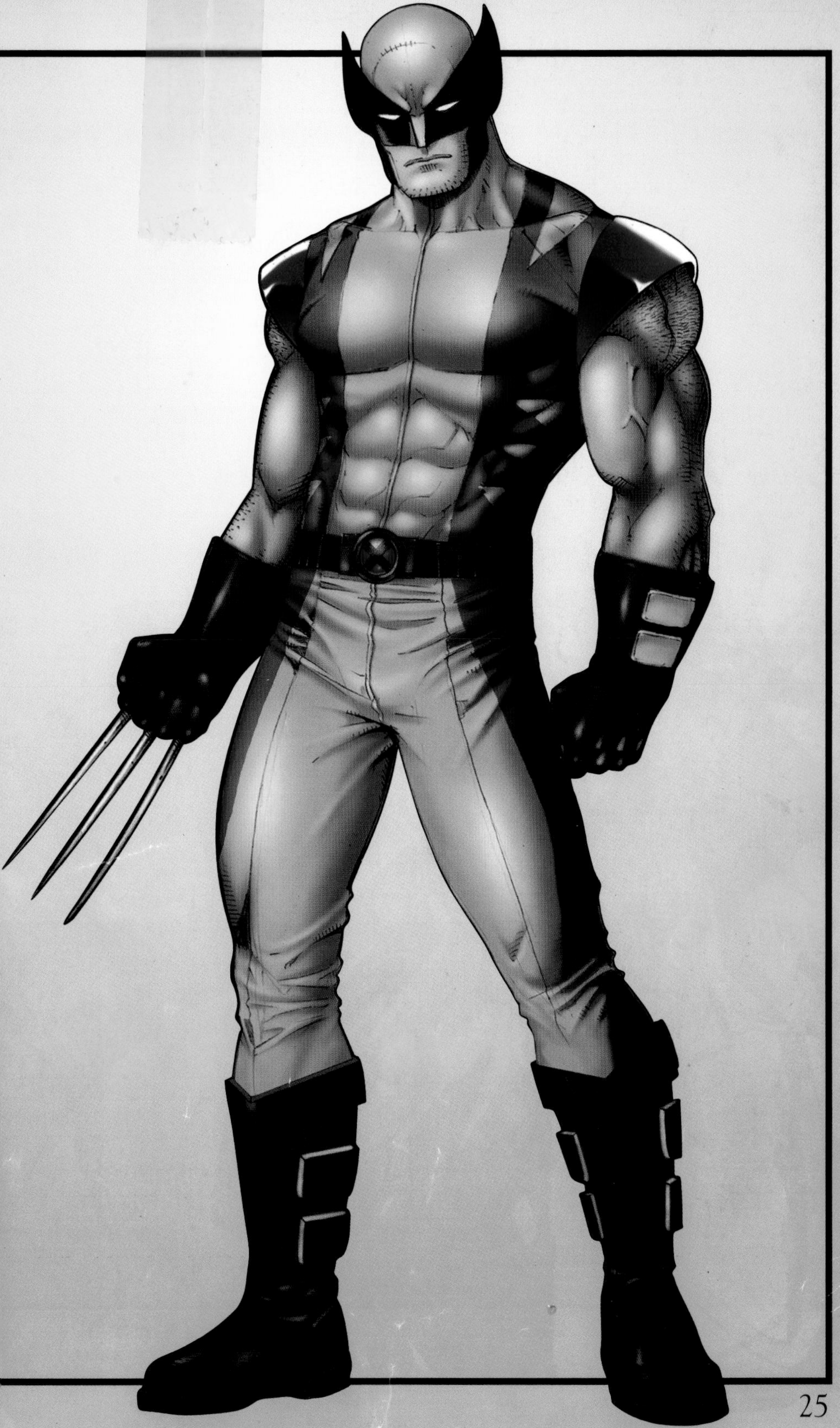

Rogue used to belong to
the Brotherhood of Evil Mutants,
the X-Men's greatest enemies.
Then she swapped sides and
joined the X-Men.

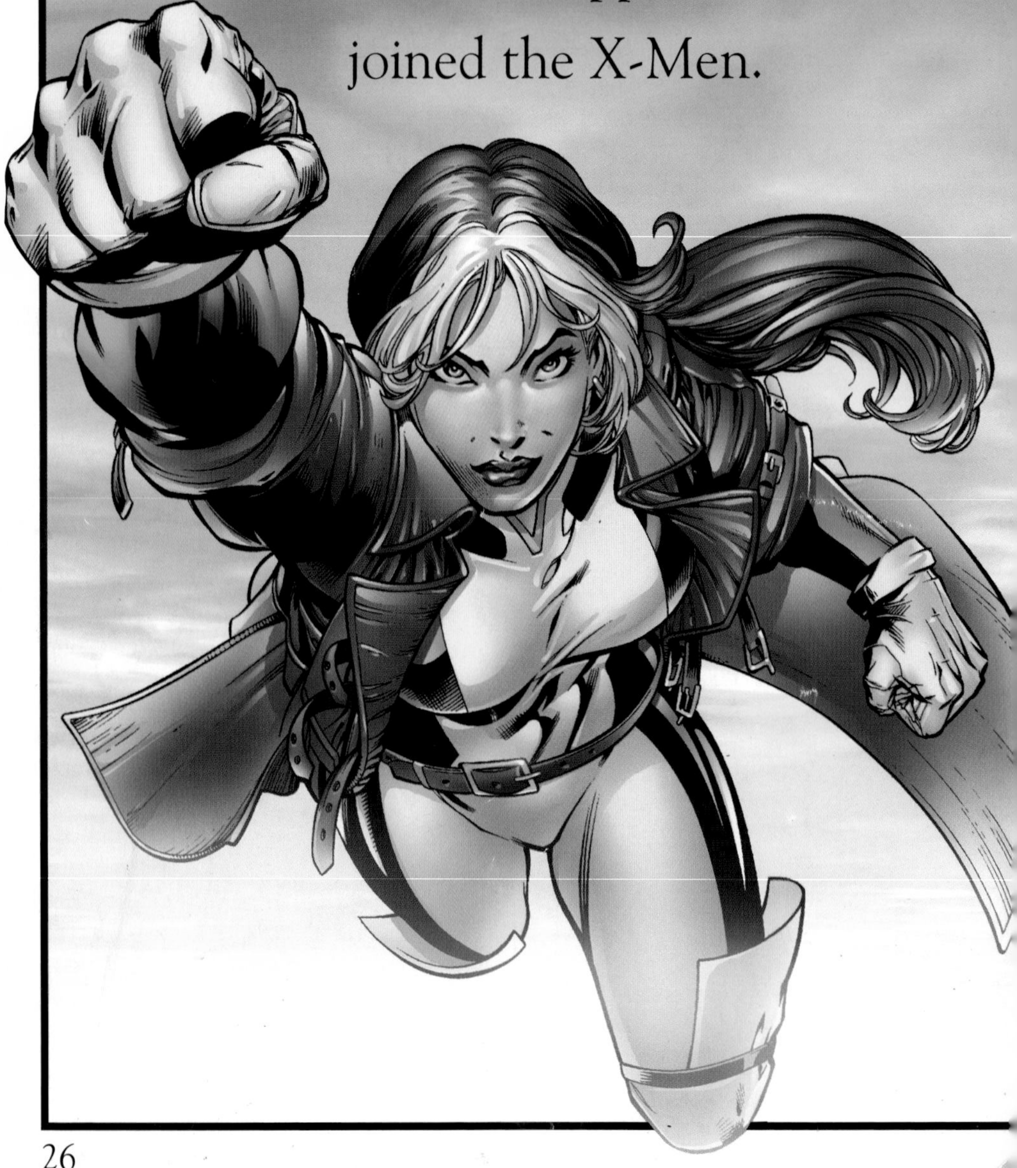

One time, Rogue took on Wolverine's powers.

When Rogue touches someone,
they become lifeless.
She takes on all their thoughts and
powers for a short time.
She wears gloves in case
she touches someone by accident.

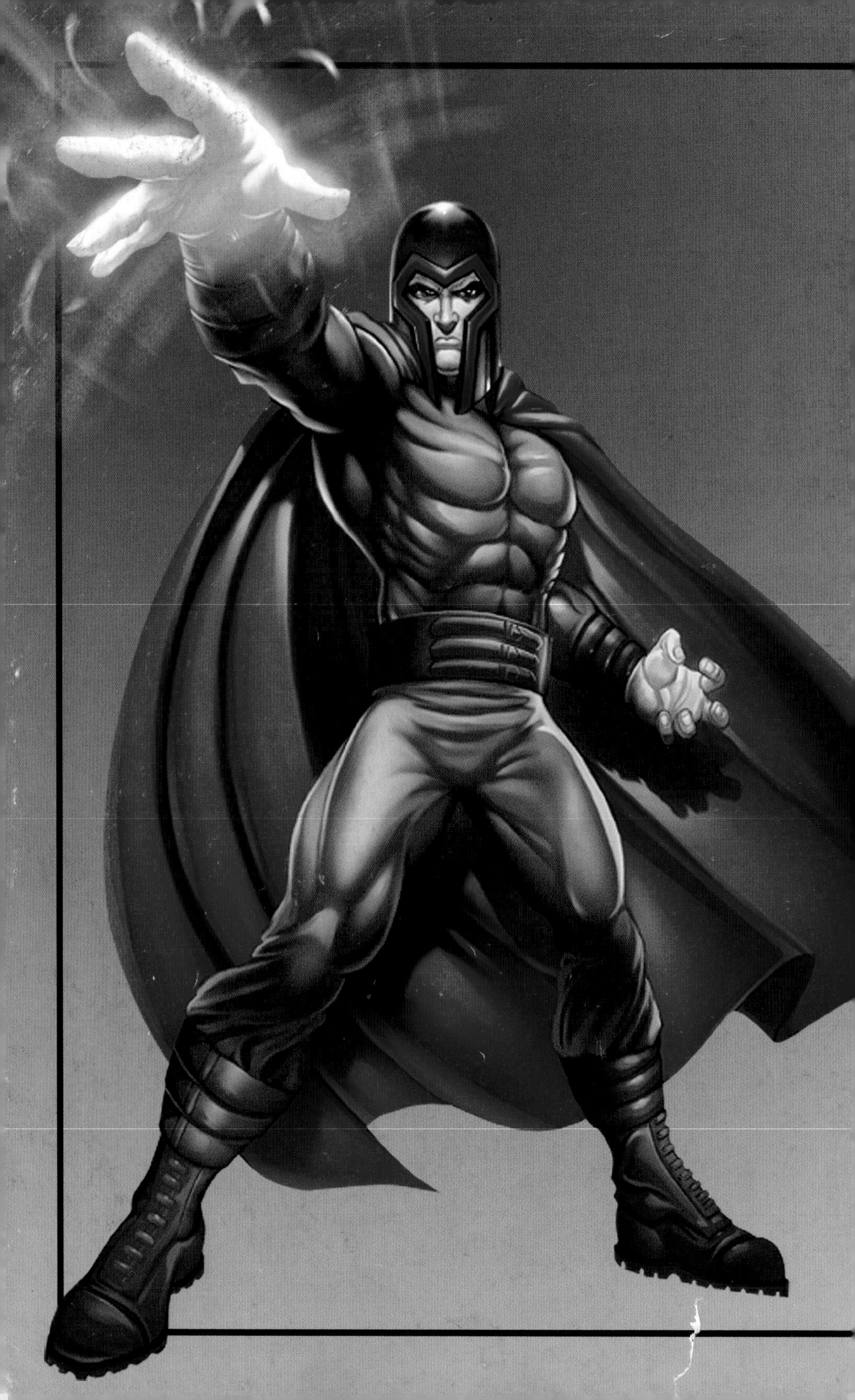

Magneto (MAG-KNEE-TOE) has strong magnetic powers and can lift enormous, heavy objects.

Magneto is the X-Men's biggest enemy.
He believes mutants should use their powers to take over the world.

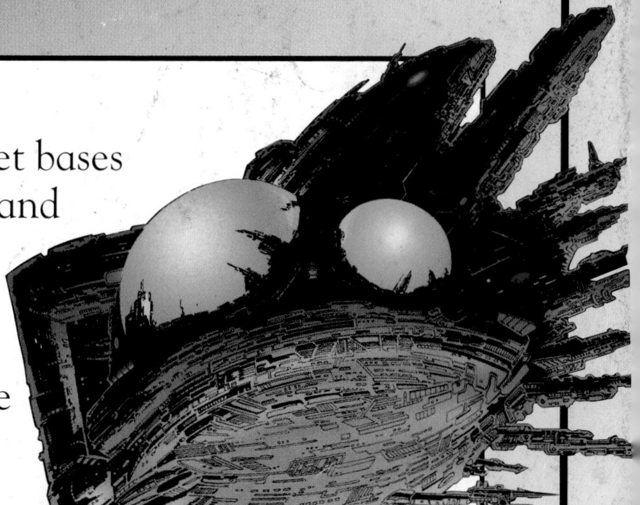

Hideouts
Magneto has secret bases around the world and in outer space. One of his main bases is on an asteroid, a massive rock that circles the Earth.

Magneto led a band called
the Brotherhood of Evil Mutants.
One member, known as Toad,
could leap very high.

Other members were Mastermind,
who could make things that were
not real look real, and Quicksilver,
who could move very fast.

Later, the mutant Mystique (MISS-TEEK) ran her own Brotherhood. The members of her team included Avalanche, who could make earthquakes, and Destiny, who could see into the future.

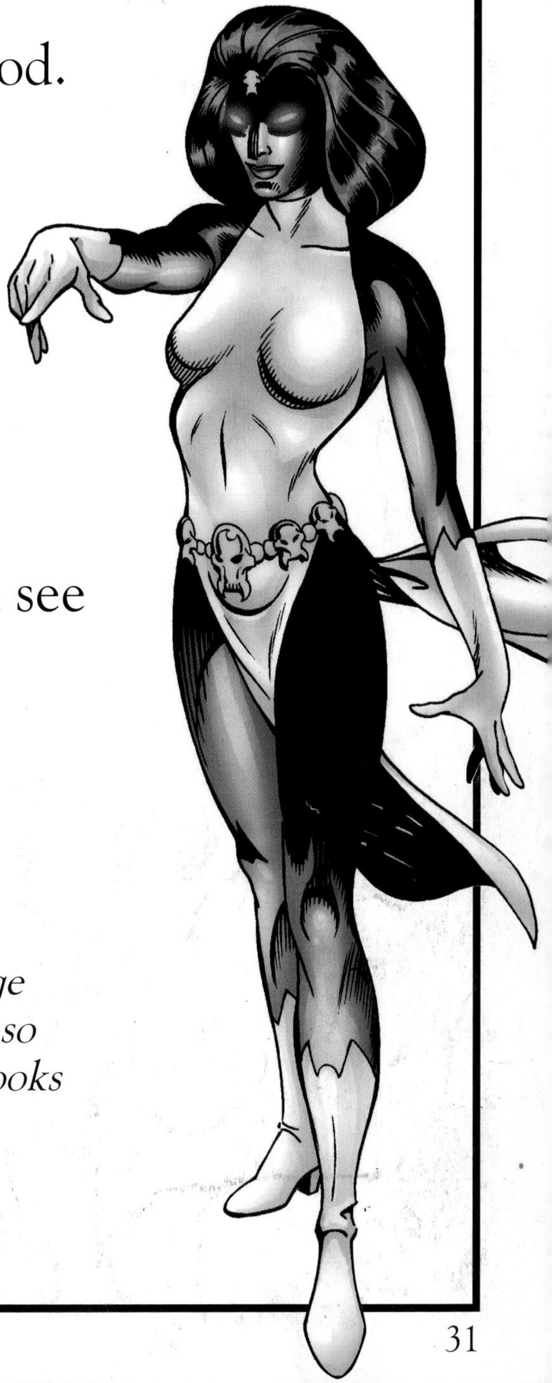

Mystique can change her shape so that she looks like other creatures.

Fascinating Facts

When the X-Men member
Banshee screams,
the sound can shatter steel.

Archangel's wingspan is
16 feet (5 meters)—
the length of
an elephant.

When he is fighting,
Nightcrawler can hold
a sword with his tail.

The strongest of
the X-Men is Colossus.
He can destroy a tank
with his bare hands.

Magneto's asteroid base
is called Avalon.
It is 150 miles
(250 kilometers) above
the Earth.

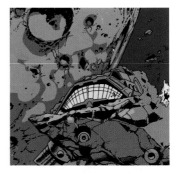

Index

READERS

My name is

_____

I have read this book

Date

_____